DATE DUE			

BUFFALO
BILLS

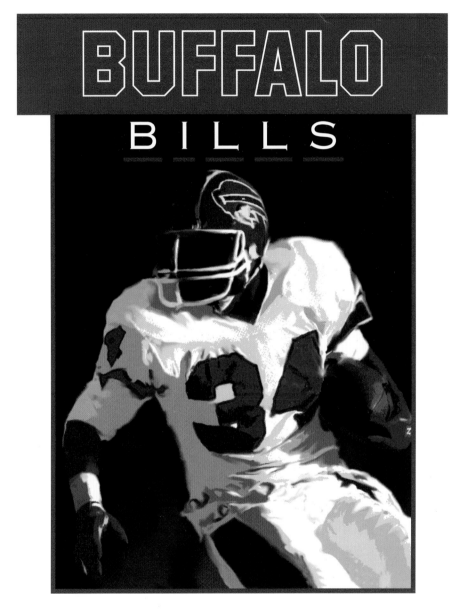

STEVE POTTS

CREATIVE EDUCATION INC.

Published by Creative Education, Inc.
123 S. Broad Street, Mankato, Minnesota 56001

Designed by Rita Marshall

Cover illustration by Lance Hidy Associates

Photos by Allsport, Bettmann Archives, Duomo, Focus
On Sports, Photos by Sissac, Spectra Action and Wide
World Photos

Library of Congress Cataloging-in-Publication Data

Potts, Steve.
  Buffalo Bills/Steve Potts.
  p. cm.
  ISBN 0-88682-360-9
  1. Buffalo Bills (Football team)—History. I. Title.
GV956.B83P68 1990
796.332′64′0974797—dc20   90-41077
                              CIP

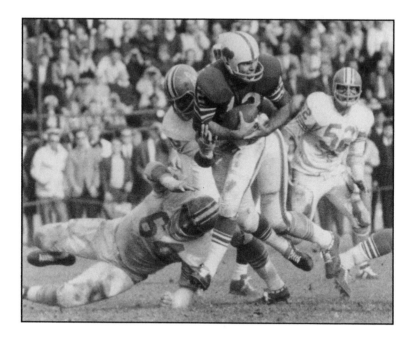

Like so many cities along the Great Lakes, Buffalo, New York is held captive every winter by huge snowfalls. The people who live in this northern city look for winter activities each year to capture their interest and fill their weekends with fun. Watching sports, especially football, is one way to survive the long, cold, snowy winters. But residents of Buffalo have not always had the chance to see professional football in their city.

When the All-America Football Conference merged with the National Football League in 1950, Buffalo lost its beloved team, becoming one of the many major American cities without a pro football club. A city that thrived on

The Bills gathered at East Aurora, NY, for the club's first training camp.

sports, Buffalo was eager to attract another franchise. The National Football League, however, was not about to grant Buffalo its wish.

Enter Lamar Hunt, the man Americans sometimes described as the "Catsup King." Hunt, a wealthy Texas businessman who made his fortune selling Hunt's Catsup, petitioned the NFL to let him start a new football team. When the league refused, Hunt contacted seven interested friends. This "Foolish Club," as this group of eight risktakers came to be known, formed a new football league, the American Football League (AFL).

One of Hunt's partners was Ralph C. Wilson, an avid football fan and Detroit business executive. Although Wilson had already bought shares in the NFL's Detroit Lions, his hometown team, he wanted a squad of his own. When he was a boy he had gone with his father to watch the Lions play, and he had always dreamed of owning a team. When Lamar Hunt suggested reviving football in Buffalo, Wilson contacted city leaders and signed a lease in November 1959 on the city's War Memorial Stadium. Today, over thirty years later, Wilson and his family still manage the franchise. He has been the club's only president and is the man responsible for returning football to Buffalo.

A TEAM AT LAST

The team did not have a winning season in 1960 or 1961, but not for lack of fan enthusiasm. Named the Bills after Buffalo's earlier team, which had been given its name in honor of Western hero Buffalo Bill Cody, the club got an unexpected "welcome home" parade on July 29,

Current Buffalo quarterback Jim Kelly.

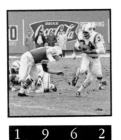

1 9 6 2

Fullback Cookie Gilchrist established a new AFL season rushing record with 1096 yards.

1960. The day before its first exhibition game, over one hundred thousand cheering fans crowded Buffalo streets to welcome their new team to the city.

The Bills' rebirth as an AFL team was directed by Garrard "Buster" Ramsey, a former guard and defensive coach for the Detroit Lions, and later Lou Saban, former Boston Patriots' coach. A man with a hot temper, Ramsey only lasted two years as Buffalo's head man. He once threatened to throw a player out the window of an airplane for performing badly on the field.

Lou Saban, who coached Buffalo from 1962 to 1965 and again from 1972 to 1976, proved more popular. Saban, who led the Bills to AFL championships in 1964 and 1965, had been a quarterback at Indiana University in the early 1940s. Like millions of other young men, he served in World War II. When he returned from the army he got a job as a linebacker with the All-America Football Conference's Cleveland Browns. Between 1946 and 1949, he played many games against the original Bills. After retiring as a player, Saban began a college coaching career in 1950. Twelve years later, he brought lots of needed experience to the young Bills.

As the Bills' head coach Saban had an amazing ability to choose players with hidden potential and turn them into winners on the field. Among those early stars were wide receiver Elbert Dubenion, fullback Cookie Gilchrist, kicker Pete Gogolak, and quarterbacks Jack Kemp, Daryle Lamonica, and Warren Rabb.

Elbert Dubenion, from small Bluffton College, became the Bills' first star. His ability to read defenses, snatch passes out of the air under pressure, and run for additional yardage earned him the nickname "Golden Wheels." It also earned him Bills' pass reception records that still stand today.

Cookie Gilchrist came to Buffalo in 1962 from the Canadian Football League and immediately proved his value as a fullback. The first AFL back to gain over one thousand yards in a season, Gilchrist, at 6'3" and 251 pounds, was nearly impossible to bring down as he sprinted toward the goal posts. In one stunning appearance against the New York Jets, Gilchrist ran for five touchdowns and 243 yards, helping Buffalo rout New York 45-14.

Pete Gogolak, signed in 1964 from Cornell University, brought a new style of kicking to the AFL. Gogolak kicked the football using a soccer-style kick. At first, the fans thought he looked funny, but his strange method was effective; Gogolak scored forty-seven field goals in his two years with the team.

The signal-calling duo of Jack Kemp and Daryle Lamonica led the Bills to five successive winning seasons (1962–1966). Instead of displaying the usual rivalry between quarterbacks jockeying for the top position, Kemp the starter and Lamonica the reliever worked smoothly, like a well-oiled machine, to create one of the league's most dangerous offensive teams.

Kemp, a 1957 graduate of Occidental College, came to Buffalo in mid-1962 from the San Diego Chargers. Although he only appeared in four games that year with his new team, he ended up in the All-Star game and produced a winning season for a team that had begun the year with five straight losses. Kemp played in Buffalo until 1969, when he retired from football. Since his playing days, he

1 9 6 4

Buffalo captured the AFL championship with a 20-7 triumph over San Diego.

The Bills' offense digs in, (pages 10–11).

*Bills' quarterback
Jack Kemp, now a
politician, was
named the AFL's
Most Valuable
Player.*

has served in the U.S. House of Representatives and as President George Bush's Secretary of Housing and Urban Development. The AFL's Most Valuable Player in 1965 now enjoys a prestigious career in our nation's capital.

Lamonica, known as the "Mad Bomber" for throwing long devastating passes, is best remembered for his ability to produce points in tough situations. Although Buffalo lost the game 26-8, Lamonica's ninety-three-yard touchdown pass in the 1963 playoff game against Boston remains one of football's most spectacular plays. Lamonica worked hard to learn the ropes at Buffalo, and when he was traded to the Oakland Raiders in 1967, his efforts paid off as he went on to lead the Raiders to three division and one league championship.

The Bills' first quarterback also should not be forgotten. Warren Rabb, a magician under pressure, became famous in Buffalo for the tricks he played with the football on October 28, 1962. With 11:57 left to play, Buffalo trailed Denver 38-23, when Warren came to life. Rabb lofted seventy-five-yard and forty-yard passes to score touchdowns, got a two-point conversion, then ran in another touchdown, all in the last quarter. These fourth-quarter heroics gave Buffalo a 45-38 win over the astounded Denver team.

Can-do Kemp! Quarterback Jack Kemp passed for 2500 yards and fourteen touchdowns.

The bubble that was success burst for Buffalo in 1967. Coach Lou Saban's departure to the University of Maryland, and trades that took Daryle Lamonica and Cookie Gilchrist, weakened the championship team. It was the end of an era, but what an era it had been. Buffalo, only seven years old, could already claim five winning seasons and two AFL championships.

REBUILDING THE BILLS

Two dismal seasons in 1967 and 1968 took the Bills to the basement of the AFL standings. Despite a few shining moments, such as on September 10, 1967, when Buffalo scored twenty points in the fourth quarter to defeat the Jets 20-17, team morale reached new lows. By 1968, the only thing to look forward to was the number-one draft pick given to Buffalo in the spring 1969 draft. It was the team's reward for finishing so low in the standings. Little did Buffalo fans or players know that their draftee, Heisman Trophy winner O. J. Simpson, would become one of football's greatest stars and America's favorite heroes.

Orenthal James Simpson, known during his playing days as "O.J." or simply "The Juice," was the object of every coach's interest when he finished school at the University

1 9 6 9

The Bills turned on "the Juice" by drafting Heisman trophy winner O.J. Simpson.

of Southern California in May 1969. While a senior, he had broken NCAA records for carries and rushing yards. When balloting was completed for the Heisman in 1968, Simpson won by the largest point margin ever. The team with the worst record in pro football in 1968, then, would be the winner of what sportswriters were dubbing "The O. J. Simpson Bowl." As the victor, Buffalo could claim the man many people believed to be the best college football player of all time.

Life had not always gone this well for O. J. Simpson. As a child in the Portrero Hill ghetto in San Francisco, he suffered from rickets, a crippling bone disease. His doctors, after fitting him with leg braces, told him he could never play football. Not a person who gave up easily, Simpson still dreamed of one day playing pro football. Along the way, however, he sometimes got sidetracked. High school friend Joe Bell recalled that Simpson wasn't always a good boy. "He wasn't any angel. If circumstances had been just slightly tilted, instead of a football   ne could have been public enemy number one." Fortunately, the time he spent in juvenile hall and as leader of the Superiors, a street gang, pointed him back in the direction of sports.

Although he starred for the Galileo High School team as a senior, low grades and the school's poor football program kept Simpson out of a major college. After enrolling in the two-year City College of San Francisco, he broke numerous national junior college rushing and scoring records, which grabbed the attention of major college coaches from around the nation. After careful consideration Simpson chose USC, the team he had watched on television as a teenager. In addition to playing football at

Tough running Jamie Mueller was quite a contrast to flashy O.J. Simpson.

Buffalo quarterback Joe Ferguson passed for 939 yards in his rookie season.

Southern Cal, Simpson was also part of the world record-setting USC 440-yard relay team. Because of this accomplishment he was often called the fastest man in cleats.

While O. J. Simpson was definitely a welcome sight in depressed Buffalo, he called his early years in a Bills' uniform the "three lost years." He felt this way because of Buffalo coach Jim Rauch's ideas about Simpson's love for running the ball. "That's not my style," Rauch argued. "I couldn't build my offense around one back, no matter how good he is." Meanwhile, Simpson felt his skills were getting rusty. He ran for less than seven hundred yards in 1969 and 1970, rarely scored, and saw his team endure three more demoralizing seasons. Simpson pondered quitting the team until Rauch picked a quarrel with owner Ralph Wilson. After criticizing two of his players, Rauch, described by Simpson and his teammates as "Satan," left the squad. The Bills endured one more losing season before Lou Saban, Buffalo's miracle worker, returned to coach the Bills in 1972.

Saban's arrival encouraged Simpson and his teammates. They knew Saban was tough and demanding, but they also liked the idea that the coach favored the running game and was honest about what he expected from his players. As he told the team after handing Simpson the ball, "There's your meal ticket. Block for him." And block they did. With 1,251 yards, Simpson won the league rushing title in 1972. Even though the team only finished with a 4-9-1 season, morale was definitely on the upswing.

Much of this change in attitude can be traced to coach Saban's creation of "The Electric Company", an offensive unit designed to turn on "The Juice." Through trades, waivers and the college draft Lou gathered an impressive

Quarterback Joe Ferguson. (page 17)

A strong defense is a Buffalo trademark, (pages 18–19).   17

Living legend O.J. Simpson made history once more by scoring an NFL record twenty-three TDs.

cast of characters. The draft brought players like Joe De-Lamielleure, Reggie McKenzie and Joe Ferguson, while other maneuvers brought Dave Foley, Mike Montler, Jeff Winans and J. D. Hill to help fill out the roster.

The Electric Company demonstrated its awesome prowess in the December 16, 1973, matchup at home with the New York Jets. On the cold playing field that day, O. J. Simpson and his teammates scored one for the record books.

Before this game, the offensive line had already given Buffalo its first winning season in six years. It had also, in thirteen games, given Simpson 1,803 yards rushing, only sixty yards short of Jim Brown's longstanding season rushing record. This was the last game of the regular season. In the icy cold that froze both hands and feet, Simpson's blockers punched holes in the Jets' defense. By the fourth quarter, O. J. Simpson, to the cheers of the fans, had broken Brown's record. He had gained 2,003 yards in one season, a record that stood until 1984. Play stopped, players from both teams congratulated him, the fans roared, and Simpson's proud teammates carried him off the field. In the press conference that followed, Simpson, never a man to grab the spotlight, gave credit to the Electric Company. They, after all, had helped him earn that 2,003 yards. As O.J. told the assembled press corps and his happy teammates, "These are the cats who did the job all season long."

The Juice and his offensive line ran the Bills to two more victorious seasons in 1974 and 1975, and Simpson's impressive list of records grew even longer. But Simpson was unhappy. The 1976 season ended with a frustrating 2-12 record for the Bills. Simpson's children, living in California, were growing up without him, and strains were appearing in his storybook marriage. Lou Saban's resignation and the departure by trade of such talents as Ahmad Rashad, Pat Toomey, J. D. Hill, and other team members weakened the well-oiled Buffalo machine. Finally, an October 30, 1977, game against Seattle left Simpson with a reinjured knee. He asked to be traded. He wanted to go home, and he wanted his chance to play in a Super Bowl.

Led by defensive back Charles Romes, the Bills boasted the NFL's best pass defense.

He got his wish in March 1978 when the Bills' new coach, former Los Angeles Rams' skipper Chuck Knox, offered to trade Simpson to the San Francisco 49ers for five future draft choices. "Home at last," Simpson chortled at his first San Francisco press conference. "Thank God Almighty, I'm home at last."

While it took him two years to rebuild his new team, Chuck Knox used his time and his five draft picks wisely to create a strong defensive. Knox already had a strong offense. Joe Ferguson had blossomed under O. J. Simpson's tutelage.

Some people felt Ferguson had football in his blood. A Louisiana native, he joined fellow Louisianans Terry Bradshaw, Bert Jones, and Doug Williams in the ranks of those few men who get to quarterback pro football teams. His Woodland High School coach, who had also coached Bradshaw, compared Ferguson to the great Pittsburgh Steelers' quarterback. Similar praise was heaped on him by Frank Broyles, coach of his college team, the University of Arkansas Razorbacks.

While at Arkansas, Ferguson perfected the long-bomb passes that made him the Bills' leading passer from 1973 to 1984. Voted an All-American during his junior year,

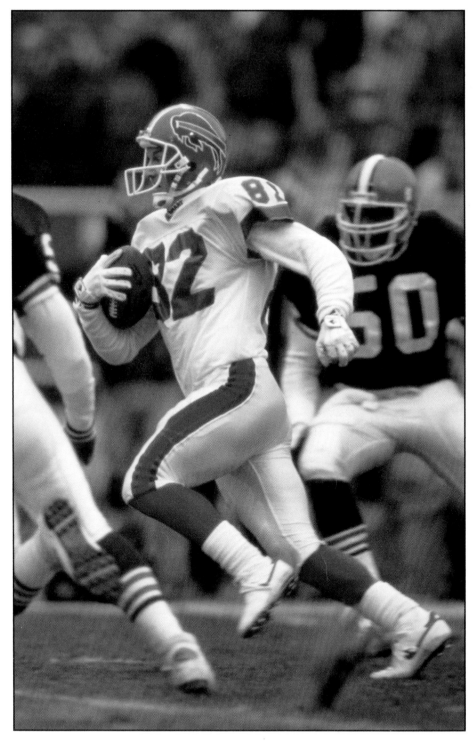

Wide receiver Don Beebe.

Ferguson was drafted by the Bills in 1973, arriving just as O. J. Simpson's greatest season began. The two became friends, and the great runner taught the young quarterback a few tricks of the game.

The other mainstay of the Buffalo offense was a young running back who came to the Bills as part of the O. J. Simpson trade. A number-two draft pick, Auburn's Joe Cribbs was a good investment. As teammate Mario Clark said, "I like to call him Joe 'Houdini' Cribbs, as in escape artist. Even when you get him in your hands, you can't tackle him. He just sort of squirts through your fingers." Cribbs led Buffalo in rushing for four straight seasons, and only O. J. Simpson ranks ahead of Cribbs in total yards rushed in a Buffalo uniform.

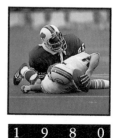

1 9 8 0

What a relief! The Bills ended their twenty-game losing streak against Miami with a 17-7 victory.

While the offense carried much of the load, Knox carefully built a solid defense to eventually support them. With high draft picks coach Knox selected Fred Smerlas and Jim Haslett, standouts at Boston College and Indiana University of Pennsylvania. Isiah Robertson and Phil Vilipiano, both linebackers, were obtained in trades with the Los Angeles Rams and the Oakland Raiders.

Knox's care in reshaping the Bills' defense and maintenance of the offense ensured their appearance in AFC divisional playoffs in 1980 and 1981. Although they didn't make it as far as the Super Bowl in either year, their last-second pass interception and ensuing 31-27 victory over the New York Jets in the 1981 playoffs convinced skeptics that the Bills were now strong contenders for the Super Bowl. The glory years seemed to be back.

A fifty-seven-day players' strike and resulting short season in 1982 upset Coach Knox's carefully laid rebuilding

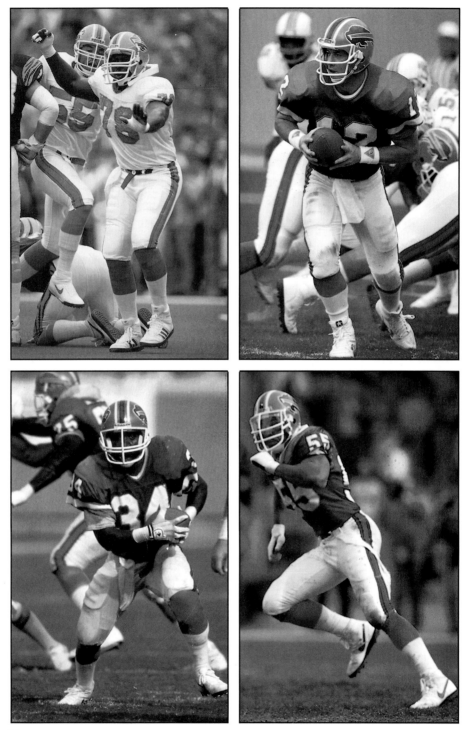

Clockwise: Bruce Smith, Jim Kelly, Cornelius Bennett, Thurman Thomas.

plans. The loss of such stars as Joe Cribbs over salary disputes further tarnished the winners. Discouraged Knox, himself, left for a new job in Seattle in 1982.

Knox's trusted assistant Kay Stephenson took over the head coaching duties. Although Stephenson was able to coach his injury-ridden team to an 8-8 record in 1983, after that he and his successor Hank Bullough weren't able to sustain the ailing Bills. The club's record sank to 2-14 in 1984 and 1985 and 4-12 in 1986. Individual standouts such as running back Greg Bell, punter John Kidd, and quarterback Joe Dufek turned in fine performances, but the team didn't rise from the division cellar.

1 9 8 6

Quarterback Jim Kelly passed for over 3500 yards in his first season with the Bills.

Accomplishing a turnaround would be up to Marv Levy, named Bills' head coach in 1986. Levy brought college and pro coaching experience, as well as work in broadcasting, to his new post. After coaching future Dallas Cowboy star Craig Morton at the University of California and serving as head coach at the College of William and Mary, Levy assisted Jerry Williams in Philadelphia and George Allen in Los Angeles and Washington. His head coaching career consisted of stints with the NFL's Kansas City Chiefs, the Montreal Alouettes of the Canadian Football League, and a USFL franchise. Few pro coaches could match his varied experience.

With this vast knowledge of the game Levy was able to quickly redirect the Bills' course. In 1987 he led them to a 7-8 record and in 1988 and 1989 he brought them to the top of the AFC's Eastern Division.

Jim Kelly pitches to Thurman Thomas, (pages 26–27).

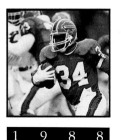

1 9 8 8

Rookie Thurman Thomas gained 881 yards while maintaining a hefty 4.3-yard average.

Levy was blessed with an impressive list of young players to work with after assuming coaching duties at Buffalo. Defensive end Bruce Smith, an All-American at Virginia Tech, was among the league's most feared pass rushers. He and linebacker Cornelius Bennett were among those to become perennial Pro Bowlers. Free safety Mark Kelso, a free agent who signed with Buffalo in 1986, had some of the nimblest fingers in the AFC. He was valued for his ability to intercept passes and run them in to score. Active in local charities, Mark was an example of what many pro players do that doesn't get them into the news. He raised $4,200 in 1988 by pledging money for each interception, fumble recovery, and tackle he made during the season.

Leading the offense was Buffalo's star quarterback, Jim Kelly, called "our future" by former coach Hank Bullough. Kelly came to the Bills in 1986 after two seasons with the USFL's Houston Gamblers. One of five brothers who played collegiate football, Kelly quarterbacked the University of Miami Hurricanes to a Peach Bowl appearance in 1980. His many records at Miami were later broken by Hurricane teammates Bernie Kosar and Vinny Testaverde. A popular figure in Buffalo, Kelly had his own radio and television shows. Like Kelso, he was also active in charity work and raised over $500,000 to help Buffalo-area children.

On the football field he was equally successful. His pass completion rate, nearly 60 percent, was one of the better marks in football. In 1989 the Bills were the NFL's second-highest scoring team, trailing only the Super Bowl bound San Francisco 49ers. Most of this success was due to Kelly's

Touchdown specialist Larry Kinnebrew.

Buffalo guard Jim Richter.

All-Pro wide receiver Andre Reed.

strong arm and the valuable assistance given to the quarterback by his teammates; Kelly was the AFC's top-rated passer, and the Bills averaged twenty-seven points a game in 1989, nearly six points better than their 1988 average. Kelly found wide receiver Andre Reed and running back Thurman Thomas often enough to make them the AFC's leading receiver and the NFL's top rusher for 1989.

It's no surprise that many observers expect great things from the abundantly talented Buffalo Bills in the 1990s. A skilled coaching staff, young players, and an endless supply of enthusiasm, ability, and hard work could add up to a successful Buffalo team. Maybe the glory days will return again, days that will earn this new Buffalo team a place in the NFL record books.